COFFEE CHRONICLES

VOLUME 1

COFFEE CHRONICLES

VOLUME 1

LATONYA CHILDS

COFFEE CHRONICLES Book Publishing
Carpentersville, Illinois

COFFEE CHRONICLES

VOLUME 1

Published by:

Coffee Chronicles Book publishing

Email: latonyacherie72@gmail.com

Latonya Childs, Publisher / Editorial Director

Yvonne Rose/Quality Press.info, Book Packager

ISBN #: 979-8-8692-3447-6

Dedication

I dedicate this book to GOD; this is where Coffee Chronicles comes from. The idea was planted by GOD, and I picked it up and ran with it! Without GOD, I am nothing!

Acknowledgements

Mommy: thank you for all that you do. You have always loved me, despite my mental illness, with all of your heart. You are my hero! Keep being you.

Leshundria: I made it baby! Thanks for supporting my dreams. Keep shooting for the stars!

Lamari: Thanks for all of your support! I am so proud of you. Keep doing what you do. The best is yet to come!

My Go-Fund-Me crew: Thanks for supporting my dream! I couldn't have done it without you!

Contents

Dedication v

Acknowledgements vii

CHAPTER 1: F.A.I.T.H.................................... 1

CHAPTER 2: H.O.P.E.................................... 3

CHAPTER 3: Menopause and Mental Health............ 4

CHAPTER 4: L.O.V.E. 7

CHAPTER 5: Series On Love............................ 9

CHAPTER 6: Mental Illnesses and Diagnoses...........11

CHAPTER 7: Bipolar Disorder:
Also Known as Manic Depressive Disorder.....................16

About the Author...21

CHAPTER 1

F.A.I.T.H.

F- Fearlessness: Lack of fear. (timothy 1:7)

A-Active: For as the body without the spirit is dead, so faith without works is dead also! (James 2:26)

I-Icarus syndrome- do not make goals you can't meet or goals that are not for you!

Soar at your own pace. Icarus' father was an inventor. They were jailed in Crete. Icarus' father created wings out of wax and feathers; and instructed Icarus not to fly too close to the water or too close to the sun. Icarus flew too close to the sun, which melted the wax on the feathers. He plunged to his death.

When the father, (God) speaks, listen stay in your lane, stay out of everything else!

Whoever gives heed to instructions, prospers, and blessed is the one who trusts the lord! (proverbs 16:20)

T-testimony: even when you are struggling, you must testify about what god is doing for you. (revelations 12:11)

H- hell-bent: determined to achieve something at all costs. (2 chronicles 15:7)

CHAPTER 2

H.O.P.E.

H- Help: To make more pleasant or bearable. To give support or assistance. (psalms 121:1-2)

O- One Way: Moving or allowing movement in one direction only. (Isaiah 43:18-19)

P- Persistence- Firm or obstinate continuance in a course of action despite difficulty or opposition. (2 Corinthians 4:8-9)

E- Effect- Cause something to happen, bring about. (Isaiah 32:17)

Be bold! (Hebrews 4:16)

CHAPTER 3

Menopause and Mental Health

Menopause- the ceasing of menstruation, usually occurs between 45 and 50 years old. No menstrual periods for 12 months

Perimenopause- changes in the menopause transition 6 years before menopause.

Symptoms

- night sweats, hot flashes
- mood swing
- vaginal dryness
- fluctuations in libido
- forgetfulness

- trouble sleeping

- fatigue (due to loss of sleep)

- anxiety

- tearfulness

- irritability

Things that could cause depression during menopause:

- having depression before menopause

- feeling negative about menopause and getting older

- increased stress

- having severe menopausal symptoms

- smoking

- not being physically active

- not being happy in, or not being in a relationship

- not having a job

- not having enough money

- having low self-esteem

Ways to feel better

- get enough sleep

- engage in physical activity at least 30 mins. A day

- set limits for yourself

- ease daily stress

- relaxation techniques

- support groups

- ask doctor about treatments: antidepressants, hormone therapy

How to get diagnosed:

Have the doctor draw for follicle-stimulating hormone (fsh)

CHAPTER 4

L.O.V.E.

L-Light: Provide with light or lighting, illuminate. Psalms 27:1

O-Overcome: Succeed in dealing with a problem or difficulty Romans 5 3-5 (message version)

V-Victim or Victorious

Victim- A person harmed, injured, or killed as a result of a crime

A person who is tricked or duped

A living creature killed as a religious sacrifice

Victorious- Having won a victory; triumphant. 1 peter 2:9-10 (message version)

E- Evolution: A process of continuous change from a lower, simpler; or worse to a higher, more complex, or better state Phillippians 1:6

CHAPTER 5

Series On Love

Agape: The highest and most radical type of love, selfless unconditional love. Christian love. Mark 12:30-31

Eros: Named after the Greek God of love and fertility. A passionate and intense form of love that arouses romantic and sexual feelings. Phillippians 2:3

Ludus: A game-playing or uncommitted love. Lying is a part of this love. People who pursue ludic love have many conquests but remain uncommitted. Romans 16:17-18 (Message Version)

Pious: marked by sham or hypocrisy

Mania: refers to obsessive love where the person is jealous or obssessive. Manic lovers view their partners as possessions. John 15:5, 2 Samuel 1:11

Philautia: self-love, self-conceit. This love can be negative or positive.

Negative philautia: the selfishness that wants pleasure, fame, and wealth beyond what one needs

Positive philautia: refers to proper pride or self-love Ephesians 3:16-18

Philia: friendship or brotherly love 1 peter 1:22

Pragma: pragmatic, dealing with things sensibly and realistically in a way that is based on practical, rather than theoretical consideration. John 14:23

Storge (store gay): familial love applies to love between family members. Can be shown to pets. Romans 12:10

CHAPTER 6

Mental Illnesses and Diagnoses

Schizophrenia a serious mental illness characterized by incoherent or illogical thoughts, bizarre behavior and speech, and delusions or hallucinations, such as hearing voices.

- typically begins in early adulthood

- drug abuse can set the stage for the onset

- a brain disorder that distorts the way a person thinks, acts, expresses emotions, relates to others, and perceives reality.

1% of the population, 2.2 million americans will develop schizophrenia.

Cognitive symptoms include trouble focusing or paying attention.

Positive symptoms include delusions, hallucinations, and catatonia, which is when a person stays in a single position for a long time.

Usually appears in the early teens or late twenties.

There are 5 subtypes of schizophrenia:
- paranoid
- disorganized
- catatonic
- undifferentiated
- residual

(romans 8:6)

Paranoid schizophrenia:

People with paranoid delusions are unreasonably suspicious of others.

This makes it hard to hold a job, have friendships, and run errands.

Delusions are beliefs that seem real to you, even when there is strong evidence they are not.

Might make you feel your co-worker is trying to hurt you.

Symptoms/criteria must be present for 1-6 months to help differentiate it from bipolar disorder. (Romans 12:2)

Disorganized schizophrenia:

- incoherent and illogical thoughts

- disorganized thinking affects speech. Can't stick to the subject.

- disorganized behavior. Unable to perform regular daily activities.

- inappropriate or lack of emotional expression.

- blank facial expressions. No contact with other people.

- usually not able to get help on their own.

Catatonic schizophrenia:

Rarer than it used to be, due to improved treatment.

Catatonia refers to a set of symptoms that can include periods where the individual moves very little and does not respond to instructions.

They can demonstrate motor activity that is considered excessive and peculiar, such as echolalia, mimiking sounds or echopraxia, mimiking movements. These symptoms are called catatonic excitement. (Philippians 4:8)

Undifferentiated schizophrenia:

Lacks the paranoid symptoms when a person is exhibiting symptoms that meet many of the symptoms of schizophrenia but does not fully or clearly fit one of the other types of schizophrenia.

- symptoms must be present for at least one month.

- this type can be challenging to diagnose.

- possible brain diseases and other diagnoses must be ruled out.

(Proverbs 3:5)

Residual schizophrenia:

- when the patient no longer displays prominent symptoms.

- schizophrenic symptoms have lessened in serverity.

- hallucinations or delusions may be present, but they are significantly decreased.

Residual schizophrenia is diagnosed by the following:

- slow movement, underactivity.

- evidence in the past of at least one psychotic episode.

CHAPTER 7

Bipolar Disorder: Also Known as Manic Depressive Disorder

It is a mood disorder:

- people may experience deep depression, with breaks of mania.

- mania-mental illness marked by periods of great excitement, euphoria, and overactivity.

- elevated mood, increased energy.

- abnormally elevated arousal effect.

Depression- a mental condition characterized by feelings of severe despondency. Typically, there are feelings of inadequacy and guilt, accompanied by lack of energy, and disturbance of appetite and sleep.

There are 5 classifications:

1. Bipolar 1 disorder-person experiences defined manic episodes.

2. Bipolar 2 disorder- a lesser mania called hypomania is paired with depressive episodes.

3. Cyclothymia- a person does not experience severe depressed or manic episodes, but still cycles through moods.

4. Rapic cycling-when a bipolar individual experiences at least 4 episodes through a year. This may be through day-to-day, difference with ultra-ultra rapid cycling.

5. Bipolar nos disorder- this is when a person does not fit in any specific category but still experiences impairment from their bipolar symptoms.

10 common symptoms

1. **Suicidal thoughts** - in the depression stage, the sufferer may feel so low that suicidal thoughts are present. Suicide rates are highest for people with bipolar disorders.

2. **Racing thoughts**

   - the mind is full of ideas, inspiration, and emotions that are hard to deal with, irregular speech patterns.

   - a person may find it hard to continue conversations for more than a few seconds.

   - thoughts may be disturbing.

3. **Loss of interest in social activities**- refusing to partake in social activities, because they are overwhelming. Isolation creeps in.

4. **Inflated ego**- showing off in public, alienating people close to them because of their ego.

5. **Feelings of guilt**- frequently feel guilty about their condition. May feel bad for not being able to control their emotions.

   Bipolar is a burden, not a choice. You should not feel guilty. Understanding your condition can help you.

6. **Overspending**- items purchased may temporarily make you feel good but are never a cure for your condition. The financial repercussions following the manic-spending episodes are drastic!

7. **Low energy**- abnormal sleeping patterns. Over-sleeping or insomnia, unable to do everyday activities: work, cook, shower, eat, care for children.

8. **Impulsiveness**- acting irresponsibly. May be interested in a whole new host of activities that they usually wouldn't dare partake in.

9. **Angry for no reason**- the frustration of being depressed manifests into anger/rage. Anger usually turns into deep sorrow quickly.

10. **Increased sex drive**- when manic, down, or non-existent when depressed.

    Statistics show that around 2.3 million americans live with bipolar disorder, roughly 1.2% of the population.

About the Author

My name is Latonya Cherie Childs. I live with bipolar 1 disorder, PTSD, and generalized anxiety disorder. I started coffee chronicles to speak to people who live like me. I intend to break down the stigmatic wall of mental illness….one brick at a time!!!